THE
WATER GARDEN

LANCE HATTATT

Illustrations by
ELAINE FRANKS
and
BRENDA STEPHENSON

This edition first published in 1997 by
Parragon
Units 13–17 Avonbridge Trading Estate
Atlantic Road, Avonmouth
Bristol BS11 9QD

Produced by
Robert Ditchfield Publishers

ISBN 0 75252 143 8

A copy of the British Library Cataloguing in Publication
Data is available from the Library.

Typeset by Action Typesetting Ltd, Gloucester
Colour origination by Colour Quest Graphic Services Ltd,
London E9
Printed and bound in Italy

"With thanks to **J**"

SYMBOLS

Where measurements are given, the first is the plant's height
followed by its spread.
The following symbols are also used in this book:
  ○ = thrives best or only in full sun
  ◑ = thrives best or only in part-shade
  ● = succeeds in full shade
  E = evergreen
Where no sun symbol and no reference to sun or shade is
made in the text, it can be assumed that the plant tolerates
sun or light shade.

POISONOUS PLANTS

Many plants are poisonous and it must be assumed that no
part of a plant should be eaten unless it is known that it is
edible.

WATER IN THE GARDEN

Water gardens can be dangerous, especially to children, and
we would urge readers to take account of this and provide a
reliable means of protection if they include water in their
garden.

CONTENTS

THE WATER GARDEN

From the simplest of trickling spouts poised to splash into a stone basin to the dignified serenity of a lake, water in the garden has an irresistible, magical quality. For some people it is the sound of a babbling brook, for others the movement of a fast flowing river, whilst for others it is the peace to be found in the stillness of a pond.

Few are fortunate enough to possess a natural water feature within the garden. For most this aquatic desire has to be satisfied by creating some element which will not only complement the surrounding environment but which can also be realized within the strict limitations of a budget.

FORMAL AND INFORMAL EFFECTS

The introduction of some form of water into the garden will, to a large degree, depend upon the existing layout of borders, lawns and paths as well as the space available. Obviously it would be both impracticable and foolish to attempt a lake within the confines of a small, town garden as it would be absurd to · place a squat, bell fountain as a centrepiece in parkland. Scale, as with all things outdoors, is vitally important.

Where the garden is designed along lines of formality, then a classic pool of symmetrical shape, rill or even canal would suggest themselves. Surrounded by quality stone paving and minimal but carefully chosen planting, the effect can be stunning. A wall mask, perhaps of a traditional lion's head, the mouthpiece acting as a water outlet, an antique cistern or an ornate fountain would all be suitable in a formal situation.

Opposite: A charming small water garden on a sloping site.

A formal pool with cascades makes a dramatic feature.

In a freer, more natural setting an irregularly shaped pond or rippling stream would be a charming addition to the garden scene. In such instances planting should be exuberant, a profusion of flowers and foliage. For a cottage garden look, a wooden barrel filled with water could be positioned in a shady corner together with an old-fashioned pump for added authenticity. On a rockery a small water course with a series of carefully contrived falls would not look out of place.

PLANTING A WATER GARDEN

Giving plants suitable and appropriate growing conditions in the garden is important if they are to

A natural, well planted stream in spring.

succeed and perform well. This is particularly so when considering planting out the water garden. Here choices must be made and decisions taken about plants which will thrive in the shallows, those which will grow in deep water, those for boggy conditions and those which simply prefer damp, moisture-retentive soil. In planning schemes these points should be borne in mind.

Water lilies, traditional surface-flowering plants for pools, have planting depths which range from as little as 10cm/4in to 1m/3ft. Other marginals, among them some grasses, reeds and rushes, will grow in shallow water of around 12.5cm/5in. The choice of plants for the bog garden, where the soil is not allowed to dry out, is wide, as is the number of

Intense greens in a garden of moisture-loving subjects.

plants which will enhance the areas surrounding pond or stream.

Where plants are to be submerged a suitable planting basket should be used. Readily available, these are of plastic construction with fretted sides to allow for expansion of roots. If the compost or soil to be used is light and friable, then the sides of the basket can be lined with old hessian sacking or coarse cloth to prevent spillage. Once filled containers may easily be lowered into place by means of cord or stout string passed through the upper holes.

CARE AND MAINTENANCE

Pools and ponds are subject to free-floating algae which flourish in sunlight and where there are high levels of mineral salts present in the water. To reduce this problem oxygenating plants, which absorb mineral salts and cast shade, should, according to variety, either be tossed onto the surface or submerged.

The majority of plants for the pond or water areas will die down naturally during the dormant season.

Water has a calming effect.

Rushes with hollow stems should not be cut down below the water line, to prevent the stalks filling with water and the plant drowning. Where trees shed leaves into the water these should be collected and removed where possible to limit pollution.

Fish should not be fed in winter. At a time when ice may pose a threat it is advisable to float a rubber ball or a piece of wood on the surface of the water to reduce the pressure naturally exerted by the ice. In severe conditions a pan of boiling water placed on the surface will melt through the ice to release any toxic gases which may have built up.

During the colder months it is worth disconnecting any pumps to be serviced, cleaned and stored in readiness for the coming season. Periodically ponds and pools should be emptied to allow for thorough cleaning and routine maintenance work.

1. PONDS

MAKING *a* POND

FEW GARDENS need be without a natural looking pond. Positioned in a quiet corner or as a dominant feature, it breathes life into the garden creating atmosphere and character. Once installed it becomes a near fixture. It is, therefore, necessary to position it correctly from both an aesthetic and horticultural point of view.

Flag iris, rushes and large-leaved foliage plants surround this peaceful pond. Lush plantings mask the edges generating visual interest as well as giving cover for wildlife. The unplanted water surface allows for attractive reflections to be seen.

Carefully positioned stone edging follows the line of the hedge which encloses this pond garden.

This pool garden relies heavily upon sweeps of close planting to achieve its effect.

Positioned within a walled garden where the heat is trapped, this beautifully planted pond forms a cool oasis.

Bold plantings of *Alchemilla mollis* mask this pond's edge whilst the royal fern (*Osmunda regalis*) adds contrast of form.

SITING A POND

Within a garden situation a pond needs to blend in with its surroundings to appear, as far as possible, at one with nature.

A low point in the garden should be chosen, and one which allows room for generous marginal plantings.

A site enjoying a good measure of sunlight will ensure that both fish and aquatic plants thrive. The proximity of deciduous trees and shrubs will make for unwanted shade, whilst fallen leaves left to rot on the bottom of the pond will release harmful gases.

Caught in a moment of bright sunshine, this well-sited garden pool looks particularly inviting.

Closely mown grass borders one side of this pond. In comparison the other is thickly planted.

A great sense of peace and calm is achieved in this attractively planted, mature pond garden.

◆ *Conifers give scale and make for year-round interest.*

Pool liners are a flexible method of creating a pond to almost any size and shape. Although a number of cheaper liners, such as polythene and PVC, are on the market, the initial outlay for a quality rubber or butyl liner will more than repay itself for its appearance and durability.

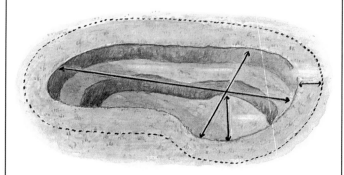

Measuring the Pond

Irregularly shaped pools should be treated as rectangles for the purpose of measuring. The measurements to be taken are: length, width, depth and overlap (the overlap is the amount of liner required to secure it firmly to the ground – approximately 45cm/1½ft). The quantity of liner needed will be:

(2 × depth + length + 2 × overlap) × (2 × depth + width + 2 × overlap)

Excavating the Site

Dig out the pool to the desired shape and size. Remove any sticks or stones likely to puncture or damage the liner. Cover the base of the pond and the marginal planting shelves with a layer of sand to a depth of 2.5cm/1in. This will afford the liner added protection. Wads of saturated newspaper may be used to line the sides.

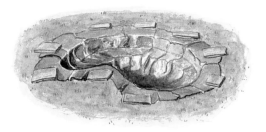

PLACING THE LINER

The butyl liner should be stretched over the excavated pond. Slabs or bricks may be used at this stage to secure the liner in place in readiness for filling with water.

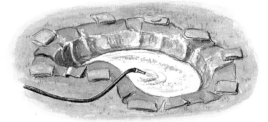

FILLING THE POND

As the pond begins to fill, major creases should be pulled out. Once full, surplus edging material may be cut away, but you will need to ensure that sufficient overlap remains, which you can conceal under edging slabs.

FINISHING OFF

Because of the non-toxic quality of pool liners, the pond may be put into immediate use. Plants may be added and fish, if required, may be introduced.

PUDDLED CLAY IS THE ULTIMATE in pond linings but it is a specialist technique requiring appropriate soil and conditions. Most people are content to use either a butyl liner or a ready-made shape. Moulded ponds are available generally in weather-resistant plastic or fibreglass. They are not made in very large sizes but are a sensible choice for a small rock pool or a feature in a small garden.

Preformed pools are ideal for even the smallest gardens. This one has been concealed beneath a naturalistic setting of slate rocks.

◆ *The water-spout is powered by an electric pump.*

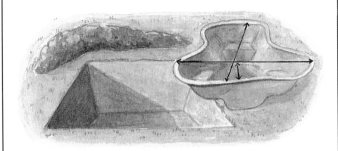

INSTALLING A PREFORMED POND

1. Excavate a large, rectangular hole which, when complete, will comfortably accommodate the pond. This hole will be greater than the length, width and depth of the pond to allow for adequate backfilling.

2. Spread a layer of sand to a depth of 2.5cm/1in across the bottom of the hole. Install the pond, supporting it where necessary with wedges which will later be removed as backfilling takes place. The pond should be set at least 2.5cm/1in below ground level to allow for any lifting.

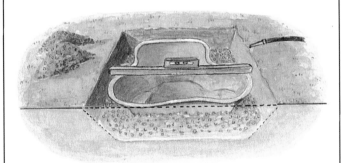

3. Check with a spirit level and commence backfilling. Continue at intervals to check that the pond is level. Firm soil around the pond to eliminate air pockets.

4. Add water whilst backfilling continues. This should result in a stable, level pond. Once full, planting may take place and the disturbed surroundings can be restored.

SOME GARDENS simply do not have
space for a pond of any real size.
However, it is still possible to include
a small feature in the form of a
sunken barrel, tank, trough or suitable
container, all of which can be adapted
to hold water.

This inviting area could well be termed a pool patio. Water,
hard and soft landscaping are given equal weight.

◆ *Garden ornaments need not be expensive. Good, reasonably
priced reproductions are easily obtained.*

A wall spout is used here above stone troughs to create an interesting, effective water feature.

Nothing could be simpler than this metal basin used as a container for water lilies.

This arrangement of mask, trough and lead-type urns shows how a completely symmetrical arrangement can be broken to advantage by the use of plants. The lion mask, centrally placed, is allowed to just peek out from his ivy hiding-place.

Caltha palustris The marsh marigold's flowers are carried above dark green leaves. ○, 30 × 45cm/ 1 × 1½ft

◆ *Ideal for edging ponds.*

***Caltha palustris* 'Flore Pleno'** is a double form of the marsh marigold forming splendid clumps. ○, 30 × 30cm/1 × 1ft

Lysichiton camtschatcensis boasts a white spathe. They are easily raised from seed but take some years to flower. 75 × 60cm/2½ × 2ft

***Zantedeschia aethiopica* 'Crowborough'** A spectacular plant whose white flowers are stunning. 60 × 60/2 × 2ft

***Geum rivale* 'Album'** (Water avens) is unfussy about situation but looks very effective with marginal plants. 60 × 60cm/2 × 2ft

Marginal Plantings

Exciting results are achieved when plants of differing form and texture are used at the margins of the pond. As well as concealing any unsightly edges, marginals act as a link between plants growing in the water and those at the pondside.

Growing in the shallows at the pond's edge is the handsome, North American pickerel weed, **_Pontederia cordata_**, its shaped foliage contrasting with that of **_Iris laevigata_**. Creeping along the edges is the cheerful little hybrid **mimulus**.

Filipendula purpurea alba
A meadowsweet splendidly
at home in a waterside
setting. 1.2 m × 45cm/
4 × 1½ft

Filipendula rubra This form
of meadowsweet deserves a
prominent place in the
pond garden. 2 × 1.2m/
6 × 4ft

Lysimachia punctata will
rapidly colonize an area but
is exceedingly useful for
difficult situations.
75 × 60cm/2½ × 2ft

**Rodgersia pinnata
'Superba'** An absolutely
lovely form. Plant in
numbers for a strong
accent. 1 × 1m/3 × 3ft

Persicaria (syn. **Polygonum**)
bistorta forms striking
clumps of pink flowers
when grown well in moist
soil. 75 × 60cm/2½ × 2ft

Iris **'Holden Clough'** is particularly effective placed in front of *Carex elata* 'Aurea'. 75 × 75cm/ 2½ × 2½ft

Houttuynia cordata **'Chameleon'** A showy groundcover perennial with small white flowers that spreads. ○, 10cm/4in

Trillium grandiflorum Patience is required as the beautiful wake-robin is slow to establish. ●, 38 × 30cm/ 15 × 12in

Aruncus dioicus **'Kneiffii'** A form of goat's beard which is not dissimilar to an astilbe. 1 × 1m/3 × 3ft

Astilbe **'Granat'** is not at all out of place when positioned among some of the red-hued primulas. 1 × 1m/3 × 3ft

Astilbe **'Deutschland'** in common with other astilbes is particularly happy in moisture-retentive soil. 1 × 1m/3 × 3ft

INTRODUCING FISH

Avoid tipping the fish directly into the water. Rather, allow the bag in which they were sold to float on the pond's surface until the water temperature of the bag is similar to that of the pond. Feed at once although it may be some time before the fish will appear regularly for feeding. To begin with, their inclination will be to hide.

The **common goldfish**, a member of the carp family, is the most popular of all fish for the garden pool. It is hardy, surviving even bad winters outside, though it needs water at least 45cm/1½ft in at least a part of its pond. It breeds easily, though not until it has reached a length of about 12.5cm/5in.

WINTER WEATHER

Fish will survive winter months without feeding, their body processes slowing down to adjust to the cold. In prolonged icy weather, surface ice may be melted by holding a container of boiling water on the pond. This will release any harmful gases trapped under the ice that could harm the fish. Never resort to more violent methods of breaking ice.

FISH

FOR MANY, A POND WITHOUT FISH is incomplete. Indeed, ornamental fish do provide a decorative element in the water garden as well as helping to control some of the insect pests to be found in and around water. The most popular choice remains goldfish, with bronze carp coming a close second. Additionally, shubunkins, common carp, orfe, rudd and roach will all live happily side by side in the larger pond.

REGULAR FEEDING

A correctly balanced pond that is not over-populated with fish will contain sufficient nutrients in the form of aquatic life to sustain health and vigour. However, feeding fish with a good proprietary brand of food will do no harm. Fish are not greedy feeders. Only small amounts of food should be given at any one time. When colder weather sets in, feeding should cease.

The **Koi carp**, the most exotic of the hardy cold water fish, is a beautiful creature with a chunky head and body.

2. FORMAL POOLS

DESIGNING *a* POOL

SPACE, the use of compatible materials
and restrained, co-ordinated plantings
are the necessary ingredients of a
formal water scheme. Designs succeed
best where they can be tied in to some
existing structure: a walled court, a
sunken garden, a terrace, an enclosure.

A well placed seat, strategically sited pots and a canopy of
trees call for a moment's pause in a city garden.

◆ *The lush plantings associated with water create a cool, calm
atmosphere.*

An excellent use of water, stone and green foliage plants to give an air of understated elegance.

Clipped ivy and box mask the construction of this above-ground rectangular pool. Planting in the water is minimal.

This pool is the centrepiece of an enclosed, brightly coloured water garden.

This brick water feature becomes an extension of the wall behind to provide total harmony.

Close planting and the proximity of the wall convey a sense of intimacy in this shady enclosure.

Large slabs of a uniform size have been used to edge this shaped pool.

DESIGNING A POOL · 31

A raised pool such as this one would not be too difficult to achieve, for it involves little excavation.

This antique pool of basket-weave design is set in a formal area of lawn and box parterre.

Symmetry and formality combine by aligning the centre of the pool with that of the door and by the placing of the planters.

◆ *Blue paint used here on the furniture and containers is much more sympathetic than white would have been.*

FLOATING *and* DEEP WATER PLANTS

FEW THINGS ARE LESS APPEALING than the sight of a pool which is the consistency of pea soup and overrun with blanket weed. Floating and submerged oxygenating plants will, to a great extent, promote healthy, clear water. Some of these plants are chosen for a specific purpose and are therefore not especially decorative. However, others will produce flowers and be pretty in their own right.

Eichhornia crassipes (Water hyacinth) floats on the surface and produces very appealing and attractive orchid-like, blue and lilac flowers.

◆ *Unfortunately the water hyacinth must be kept frost-free. Overwinter in a container of water.*

Myriophyllum aquaticum
(Parrot's feather) thrives
beneath the water's surface
where it helps to keep water
clear.

Aponogeton distachyos
(Water hawthorn) has white
flowers with distinctive
black centres. Plant in up to
45cm/1½ft of water.

Orontium aquaticum possesses very striking, poker-like
flowers tipped yellow.

◆ *Plant in up to 30cm/1ft of water.*

WATER LILIES

WATER LILIES, *Nymphaea*, are the most desirable, decorative and coveted of all pool plants. They thrive in good garden soil and should be planted either directly into the soil on the floor of the pond or into open-sided, aquatic planting baskets.

Nymphaea **'Sioux'** The blooms start off soft yellow and pass through orange-pink to crimson. Olive-green leaves. PD 45cm/1½ft

Nymphaea **'Mme Wilfon Gonnère'** Almost fully double cup-shaped flowers, 15cm/6in across. PD 45cm/1½ft

Nymphaea **'Venusta'** Beautifully formed flowers of warm pink, stuffed with golden stamens. PD 45cm–1m/1½–3ft

PLANTING DEPTHS (PD)

Miniature lilies require no more than 23cm/9in of water whilst the small-growing varieties are happy in up to 30cm/1ft. Medium-growing lilies should have somewhere up to 45cm/1½ft of water; the most vigorous will tolerate up to 1m/3ft.

All water lilies should be planted in full sun and still water is essential for them.

Nymphaea 'Rosennymphe'
Delicately coloured with
pointed petals to its large
flowers. PD 45cm–1m/
1½–3ft

Nymphaea 'Graziella' A
cup-shaped flower with
rounded lobes above dark
green leaves, mottled with
maroon. PD 23cm/9in

Nymphaea 'Gonnère' A
fully double white water lily
up to 20cm/8in across and
bright green leaves. PD up
to 45cm/1½ft

**Nymphaea 'Marliacea
Albida'** A pure white,
scented lily with distinctive
yellow stamens. PD 45cm/
1½ft

Nymphaea 'Escarboucle' A vigorous water lily with flowers
up to 15cm/6in, their cup filled with golden stamens.
PD 1m/3ft

◆ *All water lilies will respond to division every few years in the
spring.*

Placing this delightful wall fountain would not be difficult. Its charm lies in its relative simplicity.

A charming Pan figure pipes water into the pool below in this formal setting.

A highly imaginative yet simple water feature which is thoughtfully composed and well presented.

Masks as water spouts are easily mounted onto a wall. A simple pump keeps water flowing.

This inspired and fascinating water feature enhances a sitting out area providing a cooling effect on a hot day.

FOUNTAINS *and* WATER SPOUTS

FORMAL WATER IS ENHANCED with the addition of a sparkling fountain spray. Whatever the design, a surface or submersible pump will ensure uninterrupted playing.

A fountain of cupids cascading in two tiers.

3. RIVERS AND STREAMS

BUILDING *a* STREAM

MODERN MATERIALS allow for the
installation of a stream or water course
in most garden situations. Concealing
the edges poses the greatest problem.
Over-reliance on unmatched rock and
stone diminishes the naturalness of the
feature and the end result can be
disappointing.

The sound of this babbling brook would be audible from
the painted bridge.

A watercourse can be installed by using a preformed modular unit. Better results are achieved with units that are interlocking rather than assembling different ones which can shift out of place if there is any movement of earth beneath.

A newly constructed rivulet made with tiered rock walls on either side. Soil beds between the ranks of stone will allow for planting.

Lysichiton americanus
(Skunk cabbage) makes a
spring show beside a
stream. Large leaves follow
the flower spathes.

Springtime, and this water-
filled ditch is transformed
into a mass of new season's
colour.

In this situation an entire water garden has
been artfully conceived. Water apparently
rises in a small pool built into a little rock
garden and then descends along a narrow course
to fall finally into an attractively shaped pond.

PLANTING *a* BANKSIDE

BANKSIDES are more often than not free-draining and not necessarily, as might be expected, water retentive. This point should be borne in mind when carrying out planting schemes. Although the impression to be given is of lush, damp conditions, these may well have to be contrived.

Hosta sieboldiana is seldom out of place. Bold leaves make a strong statement. ◑, 75 × 75cm/2½ × 2½ft

Asphodeline lutea (Yellow asphodel) Unusual, rather spiky flowers are set above grassy leaves tinged blue-green. 1m × 60cm/3 × 2ft

Digitalis grandiflora A lovely perennial foxglove thriving in both sun and part shade. Evergreen. 75 × 30cm/2½ × 1ft

Lamium maculatum 'White Nancy' A slowly spreading dead nettle with mottled foliage and white flowers. ◑, 30 × 60cm/1 × 2ft

◆ *There are also several varieties of dead nettles with pink flowers, such as* L. m. roseum *and* L. m. *'Wootton Pink'.*

Bergenia Bold, evergreen leaves of bergenias are invaluable for providing form and interest in the garden. 60 × 45cm/2 × 1½ft

Schizostylis coccinea All Kaffir lilies are best in moist conditions. Flowers appear from late summer. 60 × 30cm/2 × 1ft+

***Dicentra* 'Bacchanal'** All the dicentras look well with water. This one has deep wine-red flowers. 45 × 30cm/1½ × 1ft

***Iris* 'Gerald Darby'** An indispensable iris for its ability to thrive in both dry and damp situations. 1m × 45cm/3 × 1½ft

Alchemilla mollis (Lady's mantle) is a near faultless, hardy perennial plant, growing to 60 × 60cm/ 2 × 2ft.

Smilacina racemosa Creamy plumes of scented flowers are borne on arching stems throughout the spring. ●, 75 × 75cm/2½ × 2½ft

Alnus cordata (Italian alder) is well suited to damp situations. Glistening leaves and fruiting cones are a feature. 9 × 6m/30 × 20ft

Cornus alba 'Elegantissima' Variegated leaves on red stems. Hard prune to maintain coloured wood. 2 × 1.5m/6 × 5ft

Salix helvetica This small grey willow acts as a foil to other plantings. 60 × 60cm/2 × 2ft

◆ *Note the way in which leaves tone with surrounding pebbles.*

A slatted bridge as this one is not difficult to construct and is totally functional.

This bridge, used to cross a narrow brook, is little more than an extension of the existing flagged path.

Simple and unobtrusive to fit its setting. A nice touch has been to arch this stone bridge.

The design of this untreated, wooden bridge has been kept deliberately plain in keeping with its surroundings.

A notional crossing point to add interest to a tiny Japanese water garden. It is formed from split timbers laid over a curving frame.

In a tiny garden this little water feature of fall, pool and miniature bridge works well. The bridge directs the visitor around the garden.

CROSSING POINTS

AS WELL AS THE PRACTICAL ASPECT of
crossing a river or stream, bridges form
a pleasing feature in their own right.
Strategically placed, they make a
compelling observation platform from
which to view other parts of the garden.

This substantial, shaped wooden bridge, dramatically
painted Oxford blue, is designed to make a statement.
Surrounding plantings have, in the main, been restricted to
green so as not to compete with the bridge.

4. BOG GARDENS

CREATING *a* BOG GARDEN

AN AREA ADJACENT TO THE POND where the soil can be kept permanently damp is an ideal spot to choose for a bog garden. Using a quality butyl liner, creating a bog garden is approached in much the same way as for a pond.

In this situation the bog garden has been attached to a pond. A retaining wall is constructed to hold back the water on one side, the soil on the other.

A butyl liner here is used to contain a water-retentive medium suitable for the moisture-loving plants that typify the bog garden.

Hosta The full effect of these superb foliage plants is illustrated here where lime-green contrasts with blue-green. 60–90cm/2–3ft

Pink and white-flowered astilbes grow alongside *Hosta sieboldiana* making effective ground cover. 75 × 75cm/2½ × 2½ft

Euphorbia griffithii **'Fireglow'** is teamed here with the pink-flowered polygonum (persicaria). ○, 1m × 75cm/3 × 2½ft

Geum **'Red Wings'** An easy plant to raise from seed which will reward with a fine floral display in summer. ○, 30 × 30cm/1 × 1ft

Arum italicum italicum (syn. *A. i.* **'Pictum'**) Wonderfully marbled leaves appear in the autumn. 30 × 30cm/1 × 1ft

Darmera peltata (Umbrella plant) Following early spring flowers, shaped leaves develop to cover the ground. 1m × 60cm/3 × 2ft

This is a very fine example of a bog garden next to a pond. An early summer show of candelabra primulas surrounds irises and the huge leaves of lysichiton with, on the right, the golden sedge, *Carex elata* 'Aurea'.

◆ *Mown grass acts as a calm green foil to this ebullient planting.*

MOISTURE LOVING PLANTS

ASSEMBLED TOGETHER the plants most suited to the conditions of the bog garden compile a formidable collection. Beautiful iris, brazen ranunculus, distinctive primulas, retiring cardamines, exciting lobelias, the list is as varied as it is long.

Iris missouriensis A fine stand of this most rewarding, lavender-flowered iris originating in the Rocky Mountains. 60 × 60cm/2 × 2ft

◆ *Team these iris with yellow primulas for a colourful show.*

Iris kaempferi (syn. *I. ensata*) (Japanese flag) A very pretty species which is not difficult to grow. 1m × 60cm/3 × 2ft

Iris sibirica **'Soft Blue'** Siberian flags can grow up to 1.2m/4ft and spread over a large area.

Cardamine pratensis (Lady's smock) An absolutely delightful flower, opening in early spring. 25 × 10cm/10 × 4ft

Preferring moist soil, members of the *Ranunculus* or buttercup family will thrive anywhere. Seen here with forget-me-nots.

Primula **'Valley Red'** This selected form of candelabra primula is a welcome addition to any garden scene. ◑, 45 × 30cm/1½ × 1ft

Lobelia **'Dark Crusader'** is not fully hardy so in cold regions the crowns should be covered for winter protection. 1m × 30cm/ 3 × 1ft

Trollius europaeus is effective in an unbroken mass. Globe flowers are best divided and transplanted in autumn. 60 × 60cm/2 × 2ft

Senecio tanguticus produces daisy-like yellow flowers in late summer. Fluffy seed heads are an autumn bonus. 1.5m × 60cm/5 × 2ft

Gentiana sino-ornata Bright blue flowers in autumn such as these are hard to resist. For acid soil only. ○, 15 × 30cm/6in × 1ft

Lysimachia nummularia (Creeping Jenny) spreads to cover a wide area of ground. Sunny blooms are fairly constant. 15cm/6in

In this damp area care has been taken to ensure that leaf shapes contrast with each other.

◆ *The removal of dead flower-heads will keep this composition looking good.*

Mimulus The spotted face of this hybrid mimulus is particularly appealing. 30 × 30cm/1 × 1ft

Arisaema candidissimum The flower, appearing before the leaves in mid-season, is wonderfully exotic. 30 × 30cm/1 × 1ft

Mixed colours of candelabra primulas can be garish in sun. Here by a shady pool their brilliance is toned down.

◆ *A shaft of sun lights the striped foliage (on the right) of* Iris pseudacorus bastardii.

Dodecatheon meadia
(Shooting star) is a beautiful
plant for a damp spot in
partial shade. 45 × 30cm/
1½ × 1ft

Dierama pulcherrimum
(Angel's fishing rod) Tall,
spraying, evergreen leaves
and graceful bell flowers.
Up to 1.5 × 1m/5 × 3ft

A harmonious and subtle grouping for later summer:
astilbes, amongst silver and brown foliage plants.

◆ *The upright plumes of the astilbe and the pendulous brown
sedge are an effective contrast.*

GRASSES, SEDGES *and* FERNS

FOR A CONTRAST IN FORM with lower growing plants, the grasses, sedges and taller ferns live up to all expectations. Particularly prized are those with variegation in their slim, dignified leaves.

Osmunda regalis, the royal fern, will flourish in even quite boggy conditions. Leaves are good for drying. 1.2 × 1.2m/4 × 4ft

Onoclea sensibilis Although its roots are inclined to run, this fern is suitable for ground cover. 45 × 60cm/ 1½ × 2ft

Adiantum pedatum
Exquisite fronds on black wire-like stems. Hardy but enjoys a sheltered spot. 45 × 45cm/1½ × 1½ft

Ferns with very finely cut foliage are to be found in the *Polystichum* group. The fronds of this example are as intricate as lace.

This planting scheme takes advantage of these foliage plants. In the background is **Miscanthus sinensis 'Zebrinus'**, a very desirable grass for the way in which the leaves are markedly variegated. In the course of a year this will reach a height of 1.8m/6ft. Centre stage is taken up with **Matteuccia struthiopteris,** the ostrich fern, whilst at a lower level **Carex elata** 'Aurea' (Bowles' golden grass) enjoys the damp conditions. All of these plants should be cut to the ground at the season's end.

***Carex elata* 'Aurea'** This
sedge is at its best in
midsummer when its
arching stems are golden.
60 × 60cm/2 × 2ft

Carex pendula (Pendulous
sedge) contrasts well with
other foliage plants. Shade
tolerant and self-seeding.
1.2 × 1m/4 × 3ft

Stipa tenuifolia Wispy seedheads and graceful form
recommend this grass for cultivation. ○,
60 × 45cm/2 × 1½ft

◆ *Architectural grasses like this can play an important part in
most garden borders.*

Carex comans (**bronze form**) is used here to soften the edges of a gravel path. 60 × 60cm/2 × 2ft

Phalaris arundinacea **'Picta'** Gardeners' garters is undoubtedly attractive for its conspicuous variegation. It is, however, invasive. 1.2m/4ft

Spartina pectinata **'Aureomarginata'** is an elegant grass for moist soil in a situation where it has room to spread. 1.8m/6ft

◆ *Green flower spikes are hung with massed stamens of purple.*

INDEX OF PLANTS